DIY Spooky Crochet For Adults

Many Fabulously Spooky Halloween Crochet Patterns

Copyright © 2020

All rights reserved.

DEDICATION

The author and publisher have provided this e-book to you for your personal use only. You may not make this e-book publicly available in any way. Copyright infringement is against the law. If you believe the copy of this e-book you are reading infringes on the author's copyright, please notify the publisher at: https://us.macmillan.com/piracy

Contents

Crochet Heart-Shaped Spider 1

A Lovely Big Pumpkin! 7

Amigurumi Candy Corn 28

Crochet Pumpkin Pattern 37

How to crochet a witch hat for Halloween 46

Creepy Candy 56

Crochet Heart-Shaped Spider

Abbreviations:

Ch – chain

DC – double crochet

HDC – half double crochet

Rnd – round

SC - single crochet

Sl St – slip stitch

St (Sts) – stitch (stitches)

TR – treble crochet

Finished Size:

This crochet Spider is about 3.5" (9 cm) wide.

DIY Spooky Crochet For Adults

Materials:

crochet thread size 3, Aunt Lydia's

crochet hook size C-2 2.75 mm

sticky-back eyes

Instructions

Ch 4;

Rnd 1. Make all of the next stitches into the fourth Ch from hook (the first Ch made) working under both loops – 3 DC, 3 HDC, Ch 1, DC (Heart point), Ch 1, 3 HDC, 3 DC, Ch 3, Sl St in center.

Rnd 2. Ch 3, HDC + DC in first St, 3 TR in next St, 2 DC in next St, DC into each of next 3 Sts, DC into Ch-1 stitch, DC in next St (Heart point), DC into Ch-1 stitch, DC into each of next 3 Sts, 2 DC in next St, 3 TR in next St, DC + HDC in next St, Ch 3, Sl St in center.

Rnd 3. Ch 3, SC in first St and in next St,

Leg 1: Ch 10, SC in 2nd Ch from the hook and in each of next 3 Chs, 2SC in next Ch, SC in each of next 4 Chs, SC in same St where Leg was started;

SC in each of next 2 Sts,

Leg 2: Ch 11, SC in 2nd Ch from the hook and in each of next 4 Chs, 2SC in next Ch, SC in each of next 4 Chs, SC in same St where Leg was started;

SC in each of next 2 Sts,

Leg 3: Ch 10, SC in 2nd Ch from the hook and in each of next 3 Chs, skip next Ch, SC in each of next 4 Chs, SC in same St where Leg was started;

SC in each of next 2 Sts,

Leg 4: Follow Instructions for Leg 3;

SC in each of next 3 Sts, Ch 1, DC in next St (heart point), Ch 1, SC in each of next 4 Sts,

Leg 5: Follow Instructions for Leg 1;

SC in each of next 2 Sts,

Leg 6: Follow Instructions for Leg 1;

SC in each of next 2 Sts,

Leg 7: Ch 11, SC in 2nd Ch from the hook and in each of next 4 Chs, skip next Ch, SC in each of next 4 Chs, SC in same St where Leg was started;

SC in each of next 2 Sts,

Leg 8: Follow Instructions for Leg 3;

SC in last St, Ch 3, Sl St in the center.

Fasten off. If you have a small hole in the center, close it while fastening off the beginning end.

Finishing

Block your applique as necessary.

The Eyes

You have multiple options to make eyes. You can embroider eyes, you can also use buttons or googly eyes. (For babies and small children items – embroider the eyes on.)

I hope you enjoyed this crochet Spider applique!

DIY Spooky Crochet For Adults

A LOVELY BIG PUMPKIN!

Notions List: Yarn Needle, Polyester Fiber Fill or Stuffing Material of Your Choice

Cute embellishments: These little pumpkins can be plain or embellished with bows, beads, fabric or raffia, maybe a piece of vintage jewelry, buttons, lace, anything….they are so cute! I have a tutorial on how to make a Pull Tie or Tuxedo Bow. You should check it out. No glue or wire required…just whip it up and attach to your pumpkins!

Hook Sizes

H–8/5 mm = Pumpkin body

I-9/5.5= Stem

Stitch Key

SC = single crochet

CH = chain

SLP ST = slip stitch

SP = space

nxt = next

beg. = beginning

st = stitch

SC DEC = crochet 2 SC together; in nxt st, insert hook, pull up loop, in nxt st, insert hook, pull up loop, 3 loops on hook, yarn over, pull through all loops on hook

repeat between * * = repeat the sequence that is between the * * as many times as stated

x = times, will follow number, example repeat sequence 8 x or 8 times

"H" Hook

Round 1: CH 2, SC 7x in 2nd CH from hook, join with SLP ST to beg. SC. (You will bypass Beg. CH 1, and it will recede to the back of work, making the seam less noticeable)

Round 2: CH 1, 2 SC in joining st, 2 SC in nxt st, and in each st around; join with SLP ST to beg. SC (14 SC)

Round 3: CH 1, SC in joining st, 2 SC in nxt st; *SC in nxt st, 2 SC in nxt st* Repeat between * *

5 more x ; join w/SLP ST in top of first SC made (21 SC)

Round 4: CH 1, SC in joining st, SC in nxt st, 2 SC in nxt st; *SC in nxt st (2x), 2 SC in nxt st* Repeat between * * 5 more x; join w/SLP ST in top of first SC made (28 SC)

Round 5: CH 1, SC in joining st, SC in nxt st (2x), 2 SC in nxt st; *SC in nxt st (3x), 2 SC in nxt st* Repeat between * * 5 more x; join w/SLP ST in top of first SC made (35 SC)

Round 6: CH 1, SC in joining st, SC in nxt st (3x), 2 SC in nxt st; *SC in nxt st (4x), 2 SC in nxt st* Repeat between * * 5 more x; join w/SLP ST in top of first SC made (42 SC)

Round 7: CH 1, SC in joining st, SC in nxt st (4x), 2 SC in nxt st; *SC in nxt st (5x), 2 SC in nxt st* Repeat between * * 5 more x; join w/SLP ST in top of first SC made (49 SC)

Round 8: CH 1, SC in joining st, SC in nxt st (5x), 2 SC in nxt st; *SC in nxt st (6x), 2 SC in nxt st* Repeat between * * 5 more x; join w/SLP ST in top of first SC made (56 SC)

Round 9: CH 1, SC in joining st, SC in nxt st (6x), 2 SC in nxt st; *SC in nxt st (7x), 2 SC in nxt st* Repeat between * * 5 more x; join w/SLP ST in top of first SC made (63 SC)

Round 10: CH 1, SC in joining st, SC in nxt st (7x), 2 SC in nxt st; *SC in nxt st (8x), 2 SC in nxt st* Repeat between * * 5 more x; join w/SLP ST in top of first SC made (70 SC)

Round 11: CH 1, SC in joining st, SC in nxt st (8x), 2 SC in nxt st; *SC in nxt st (9x), 2 SC in nxt st* Repeat between * * 5 more x; join w/SLP ST in top of first SC made (77 SC)

Round 12: CH 1, SC in joining st, SC in nxt st (9x), 2 SC in nxt st; *SC in nxt st (10x), 2 SC in nxt st* Repeat between * * 5 more x; join w/SLP ST in top of first SC made (84 SC)

Round 13: CH 1, SC in joining st, SC in nxt st (10x), 2 SC in nxt st; *SC in nxt st (11x), 2 SC in nxt st* Repeat between * * 5 more x; join w/SLP ST in top of first SC made (91 SC)

Round 14: CH 1, SC in joining st, SC in nxt st (11x), 2 SC in nxt st; *SC in nxt st (12x), 2 SC in nxt st* Repeat between * * 5 more x; join w/SLP ST in top of first SC made (98 SC)

Round 15- 29: CH 1, SC in joining st, and in each st around; join w/SLP ST in top of first SC made (98 SC)

Note, if you would like a taller pumpkin, add more rows

here....just crochet until you are content. One of my testers added HDC rows at this point, to get the height she wanted.

Decrease rounds follow, you may start stuffing your pumpkin at this point, but there will be an opening at the end to finish stuffing your pumpkin. You will close the hole after stuffing is complete.

Round 30: CH 1, SC in joining st, SC in nxt st (11x), SC DEC; *SC in nxt st (12x), SC DEC* Repeat between * * 5 more x; join w/slp st in top of first SC made (91 SC)

Round 31: CH 1, SC in joining st, SC in nxt st (10x), SC DEC; *SC in nxt st (11x), SC DEC* Repeat between * * 5 more x; join w/SLP ST in top of first SC made (84 SC)

Round 33: CH 1, SC in joining st, SC in nxt st (9x), SC DEC; *SC in nxt st (10x), SC DEC* Repeat between * * 5 more x; join w/SLP ST in top of first SC made (77 SC)

Round 34: CH 1, SC in joining st, SC in nxt st (8x), SC DEC; *SC in nxt st (9x), SC DEC* Repeat between * * 5 more x; join w/SLP ST in top of first SC made (70 SC)

Round 35: CH 1, SC in joining st, SC in nxt st (7x), SC DEC; *SC in nxt st (8x), SC DEC* Repeat between * * 5 more x; join w/SLP ST in top of first SC made (63 SC)

Round 36: CH 1, SC in joining st, SC in nxt st (6x), SC DEC; *SC in nxt st (7x), SC DEC* Repeat between * * 5 more x; join w/SLP ST in top of first SC made (56 SC)

Round 37: CH 1, SC in joining st, SC in nxt st (5x), SC DEC; *SC in nxt st (6x), SC DEC* Repeat between * * 5 more x; join w/SLP ST in top of first SC made (49 SC)

Round 38: CH 1, SC in joining st, SC in nxt st (4x), SC DEC; *SC in nxt st (5x), SC DEC* Repeat between * * 5 more x; join w/SLP ST in top of first SC made (42 SC)

Round 39: CH 1, SC in joining st, SC in nxt st (3x), SC DEC; *SC in nxt st (4x), SC DEC* Repeat between * * 5 more x; join w/SLP ST in top of first SC made (35 SC)

Round 40: CH 1, SC in joining st, SC in nxt st (2x), SC DEC; *SC in nxt st (3x), SC DEC* Repeat between * * 5 more x; join w/SLP ST in top of first SC made (28 SC)

Round 41: CH 1, SC in joining st, SC in nxt st; SC DEC; *SC in nxt st (2x), SC DEC* Repeat between * * 5 more x; join w/SLP ST in top of first SC made

(21 SC)

Round 42: CH 1, SC in joining st, SC DEC; *SC in nxt st, SC DEC* 5 more x; join w/SLP ST in top of first SC made (14 SC)

DIY Spooky Crochet For Adults

Stop here and finish stuffing your pumpkin

Round 43: CH 1, SC DEC in joining st; *SC DEC* 5 more x; join w/SLP ST in top of first SC made, end off by pulling yarn through last st made, leaving a 2 ½ – 3 ft. tail for sewing through the center and around the pumpkin. Picture tutorial will be at the end of the pattern (7 SC)

Stem "I" Hook

Round 1: CH 2, SC 7x in 2nd CH from hook, join with slp st to beg. SC

Round 2: CH 1, SC in joining st; 2 SC in nxt st; SC in nxt st; 2 SC in nxt st; SC in last st: join w/SLP ST to beg. SC (7 SC)

Round 3 & 4: CH 1, SC in joining st and in each st around, join w/SLP to beg. SC (7 SC)

Add another row here if you would like a taller stem.

Next take the beginning tail and the ending tail, and tie them together, pulling the beginning tail just enough to flatten out and shape the top of your stem if.

Then stuff the yarn ends back up inside, and glue the stem onto the pumpkin.

You can stuff the stem with polyfil, and sew it on if you would like. I glued a stem to a pumpkin and when I didn't like the color, I thought could be pulled off. Nope! It would not come off without tearing up the pumpkin. Hot glue and yarn make a tight bond.

Tutorial on pumpkin shaping

Start stuffing and shaping your pumpkin.

Stuffing the pumpkin, but let's make that hole smaller.

You will need to close the hole once the pumpkin is stuffed to the firmness that you desire. (I like my pumpkins semi-firm. Also, use your finger to poke a hole through the center of the stuffing, so your needle can go through without getting stuck

on your stuffing)

Before you make the hole smaller, use your finger to create a hole in the stuffing in the center.

Keep decreasing until the hole is almost closed.

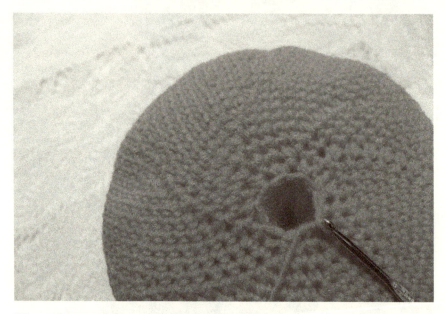

Keep decreasing until the hole is almost closed.

Keep going…when the hole looks small like this it is time to close it up.

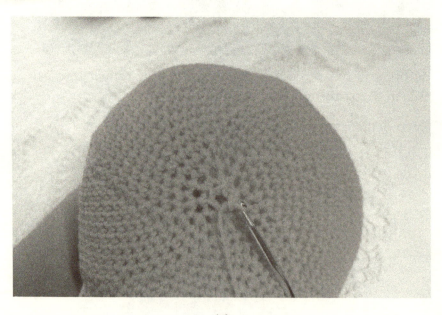

DIY Spooky Crochet For Adults

Keep going…when the hole looks small like this it is time to close it up.

Close the hole by joining with a SLP ST to the opposite side.

Close the hole by joining with a SLP ST to the opposite side.

Pull the yarn through to finish closing the hole. This is the bottom of your pumpkin. You will need a very long tail of yarn.

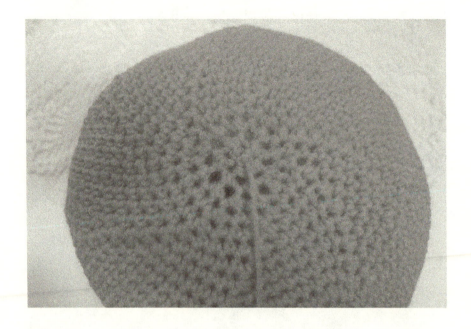

Pull the yarn through to finish closing the hole. This is the bottom of your pumpkin. You will need a very long tail of yarn.

Thread your tail into the yarn needle. or very long needle, insert the needle in the bottom center. Note the needle nosed pliers.

DIY Spooky Crochet For Adults

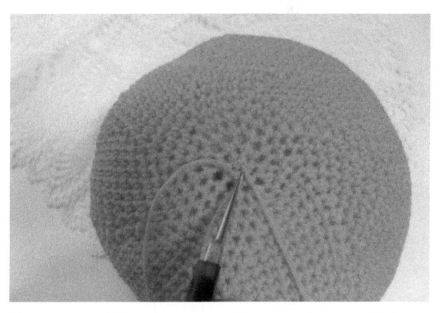

Thread your tail into the yarn needle. or very long needle, insert the needle in the bottom center. Note the needle nosed pliers.

Push the needle through the center of the bottom, to the top of your pumpkin. Since this is a larger pumpkin, you can use Needle Nosed pliers to push the needle through to the other side at the top of the pumpkin.

Push the needle through the center of the bottom, to the top of your pumpkin. Since this is a larger pumpkin, you can use Needle Nosed pliers to push the needle through to the other side at the top of the pumpkin.

Pull the yarn through the top center of the pumpkin and make a dent.

DIY Spooky Crochet For Adults

Pull the yarn through the top center of the pumpkin and make a dent.

The first dent sequence, will dent ½ of the pumpkin. You do this by wrapping the yarn completely around the pumpkin, coming back to the top, making sure your pumpkin is halved and evenly dented. NOTE: You will be inserting the needle from top to bottom during the rest of the pumpkin shaping.

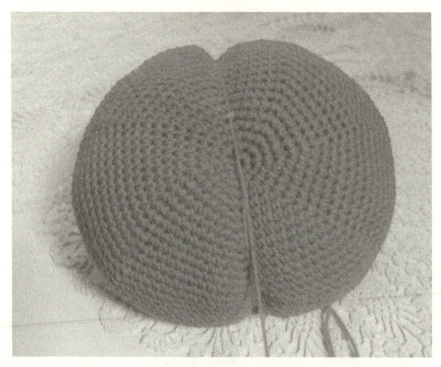

The first dent sequence, will dent ½ of the pumpkin. You do this by wrapping the yarn completely around the pumpkin, coming back to the top, making sure your pumpkin is halved and evenly dented. NOTE: You will be inserting the needle from top to bottom during the rest of the pumpkin shaping.

The rest of the dents, will be made on a ¼ of the pumpkin, instead of ½ of the pumpkin.

The following dents will be made 1/4 increments instead of half.

I use the clock method of shaping, 12 to 6, 3 to 9 and so on. (I am pulling and holding the yarn off screen to show you the dent's in the pumpkin)

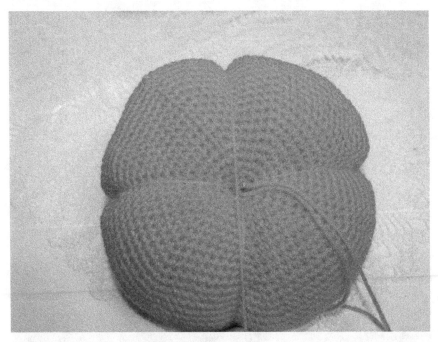

I use the clock method of shaping, 12 to 6, 3 to 9 and so on. (I am pulling and holding the yarn off screen to show you the dent's in the pumpkin)

Go completely through the top and out the center bottom of the pumpkin, pulling and shaping to make the dents secure.

Go completely through the top and out the center bottom of the pumpkin, pulling and shaping to make the dents secure.

Continue to bring the yarn from the bottom of the big pumpkin to the top, making evenly spaced dents, and inserting your needle down into the center hole at the top.

Continue to bring the yarn from the bottom of the big pumpkin to the top, making evenly spaced dents, and inserting your needle down into the center hole at the top.

You can wrap the dents twice if you choose. Sew your stem in the dent at the top of the pumpkin, or use hot glue…I like hot glue!

You can wrap the dents twice if you choose. Sew your stem in the dent at the top of the pumpkin, or use hot glue…I like hot glue!

And then embellish to your hearts content!

Amigurumi Candy Corn

I'm so excited Fall is here! I love that each season brings different colors and weather. Here in the Pacific Northwest we usually get a lot of rain but it also makes for a lot of green and pretty views!

When October hits I usually think of candy corn. I actually don't like the taste of them oddly enough, but I do enjoy their colors! Makes me think of falling leaves and the cozy warmth indoors!

These little amigurumi candy corn stuffies work up extremely fast, can fit in your hand and the best part? No sewing involved! I made some with cute little expressions but they are also super cute just as is!

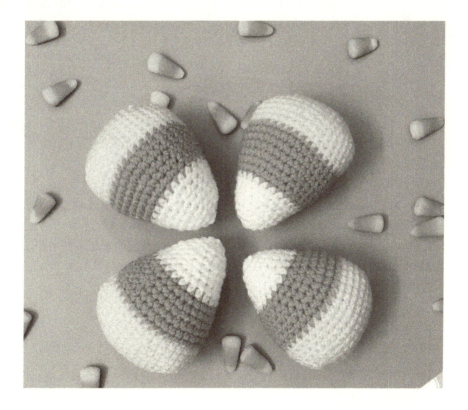

As I mentioned above, these can also be made without the facial features!

Most amigurumi patterns start with a magic circle but I really wanted to keep the oval shape that candy corn has. The start of this candy corn is very similar to the snout on the amigurumi cow pattern! We will work both sides of the chain to create an oval shape and that will be our base!

With the oval shape it made the color changes occur at the side, which I really enjoyed! They were less noticeable and if using the invisible color change method it makes it even more seamless. I have a picture tutorial for you below if you haven't used this method before!

Pattern

- Get an ad-free printable version in my Etsy or Ravelry store!

You may make and sell items made from this pattern but please do not sell, share or reproduce the actual pattern. If you sell finished items online (Etsy, etc) please provide a link to the pattern and credit to me as the designer, thank you. I hope you enjoy this pattern!

Materials

Size 4 worsted weight yarn in yellow, orange, and white (approx. 25g total)

Pink yarn for the cheeks (optional)

3.5 mm crochet hook 9mm safety eyes

Black crochet/embroidery thread for eyelashes, mouth, and

eyebrows (optional)

Scissors

Tapestry needle Stuffing

Stitch markers (scrap yarn or a paper clip works well too)

Abbreviations: US terminology

SC- Single crochet

INV DEC- Invisible decrease

St(s)- Stitch(es)

Each candy corn measures about 4 inches tall.

*Slowly stuff as you go, you want it to be firm but not stretched. You will be working in the round, I like using a stitch marker at the beginning of each round.

How to Make An Invisible Color Change

1. When completing the last stitch before your color change, insert your hook into your stitch, yarn over with the first color and pull through.

2. Drop your first color and use your new color to yarn over and finish the stitch by pulling through all loops on your hook.

You now have your new color on your hook. I like to tie off my old color here as we won't need to carry it.

3. When starting your next round, complete your first stitch as a slip stitch instead of a SC. When you come back around to start your next round be sure to SC into your slip stitch just as if it were a regular stitch.

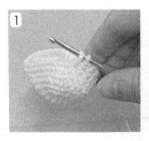
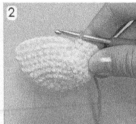
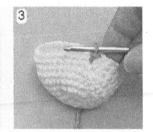

Let's get started!

With yellow, chain 10

Round 1: SC in the 2nd chain from hook, SC in the next 7 chains, 3SC in the last chain; working down the other side of the foundation chain (see picture), SC in the next 7 chains, complete 2SC in the last chain (which is also the first chain we started with) (20)

DIY Spooky Crochet For Adults

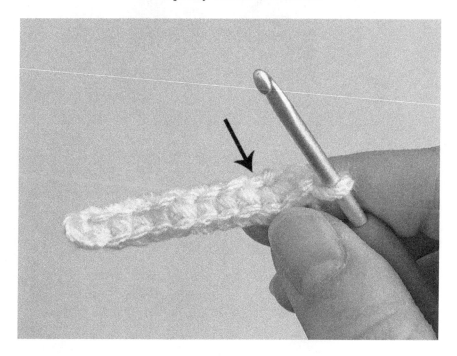

Round 2: 2SC in the first st, SC in the next 7 sts, 2SC in each of the next 3 sts, SC in the next 7 sts, 2 SC in each of the last 2 sts (26)

Round 3: 2SC in the first st, SC in the next 10 sts, 2SC in each of the next 3 sts, SC in the next 10 sts, 2SC in the last 2 sts (32)

Round 4: 2SC in the first st, SC in the next 12 sts, 2SC in each of the next 4 sts, SC in the next 12 sts, 2SC in the last 3 sts (40)

Rounds 5-6: SC around (40)

Round 7: SC in the first 8 sts, INV DEC in the next, rep around

(36)

Round 8: SC around (36) Change to orange

Rounds 9-11: SC around (36)

Round 12: SC in the first 4 sts, INV DEC in the next, rep around (30)

Round 13: SC around (30)

Round 14: SC in the first 3 sts, INV DEC in the next, rep around (24) Change to white

Rounds 15-16: SC around (24)

Here we will add our facial features: (optional)

Insert the eyes 4 stitches apart between rounds 12-13. Add cheeks, eyelashes, eyebrows and smile to your liking.

Round 17: SC in the first 2 sts, INV DEC in the next, rep around (18)

Rounds 18-19: SC around (18)

Round 20: SC in the first st, INV DEC in the next, rep around (12)

Round 21: SC around (12)

Be sure to finish stuffing to your liking before closing

Round 22: INV DEC in each st around (6)

Fasten off and sew remaining hole closed.

DIY Spooky Crochet For Adults

Crochet Pumpkin Pattern

Pattern

You can also shop the ad-free PDF version in my Etsy or Ravelry shop!

Materials -

95 yards size 4 worsted weight cotton yarn (pumpkin)

Small amount of beige yarn (stem)

4 mm crochet hook

Scissors

Tapestry needle

Stuffing

Stitch markers

Abbreviations- US terminology

CH – Chain

MC – Magic circle

SC- Single crochet

SC INC- Single crochet increase

HDC – Half double crochet

SL ST – Slip stitch

ST(S)- Stitch(es)

Finished pumpkin measures approximately 4.5 inches tall and 4 inches wide.

Gauge is not critical for this project.

You may make and sell items made from this pattern but please do not sell, share or reproduce the actual pattern. If you sell finished items online (Etsy, etc) please provide a link to the pattern and credit to me as the designer, thank you. I hope you enjoy this pattern!

NOTES -

- Leave a long tail (approximately 10 inches) at the beginning and end of your piece, we will use these for assembling the pumpkin.

- CH 1 at the end of each row does not count as a stitch.

- For ease of pattern each row of the pumpkin will start with a HDC and end with a SL ST. This will create an even texture.

DIY Spooky Crochet For Adults

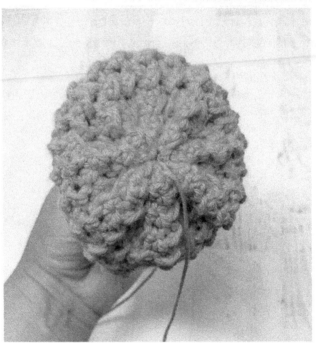

CH 33

Row 1: *HDC in the 2nd CH from your hook, SL ST in the next*, *repeat until you reach the end of the row, CH 1 and turn (32)

Row 2: *HDC in the first ST, SL ST in the next*, *repeat until the end of the row, CH 1 and turn (32)

Rows 3-45: Repeat row 2

Fasten off leaving a long tail for sewing.

Stem –

Round 1: Create a magic circle with 6 SC

Round 2: SC INC in each ST (12)

Rounds 3-7: SC around (12)

Fasten off leaving a long tail for sewing.

Assembly –

- Fold your pumpkin panel in half, lining up your beginning row with your last row. With your tapestry needle whip stitch across to close. I placed my needle through the inside loops to create a more solid seam.

- You now have a tube. Weave your needle in and out of the top portion, cinch tight to close and secure with a knot. This will be the base of your pumpkin.

-

Fill your pumpkin ¾ full of stuffing and weave through the top in the same fashion as above. Cinch tight to close and push your needle through the middle to the bottom base. Pull tight to give a sunken look and secure with a knot. Fasten off and weave in your end.

- Lastly, lightly stuff your stem and sew onto the top of your pumpkin.

How to crochet a witch hat for Halloween

Witch creation

This Halloween, whip up an easy witch hat and enchant everybody!

Check out these step-by-step instructions on how to make your own crocheted witch hat.

Level:

Easy

Size:

45 cm (17.5 inches) long and 52 cm (21 inches) wide (head circumference)

Abbreviations

Report ad

ch: chain

sc: single crochet

scinc: single crochet increase

sctfl: single crochet through front loops

hdc: half double crochet

dc: double crochet

p: picot stitch

st(s): stitch(es)

Materials

Worsted-weight yarn in black (about 120 grams) and purple (about 30 grams) for the hat; small amount of white for spider web

Size 3.5 (E) and 4.00 (G) crochet hook

Yarn needle

Stitch marker (optional)

Pattern notes

Tension is not critical for this project.

Work stitches continuously in a spiral without closing off each round with a slip stitch. It may help to use a stitch marker in the first stitch of each round, moving it up as you work.

The pattern

Witch hat

DIY Spooky Crochet For Adults

With black yarn and 4.00 mm (G) hook

Ch2.

or

Make a magic loop.

R1: 6 sc in 2nd ch from hook. (6)

R2: 1 hdc in each st around. (6)

R3: 2 hdc in each st around. (12)

R4-5: 1 hdc in each st around. (12)

R6: *2 hdc in next st, 1 hdc in next st* repeat from* 6 times. (18)

R7-8: 1 hdc in each st around. (18)

Report ad

R9: *2 hdc in next st, 1 hdc in each of next 2 sts*, repeat from*

6 times. (24)

R10-11: 1 hdc in each st around. (24)

R12: *2 hdc in next st, 1 hdc in each of next 3 sts*, repeat from* 6 times. (30)

R13-14: 1 hdc in each st around. (30)

R15: *2 hdc in next hdc, 1 hdc in each of next 4 sts*, repeat from* 6 times. (36)

R16-17: 1 hdc in each st around. (36)

R18: *2 hdc in next st, 1 hdc in each of next 5 sts*, repeat from* 6 times. (42)

R19-20: 1 hdc in each st around. (42)

R21: *2 hdc in next st, 1 hdc in each of next 6 sts*, repeat from* 6 times. (48)

R22-23: 1 hdc in each st around. (48)

R24: *2 hdc in next st, 1 hdc in each of next 7 sts*, repeat from* 6 times. (54)

R25-26: 1 hdc in each st around. (54)

R27: *2 hdc in next st, 1 hdc in each of next 8 sts*, repeat from* 6 times. (60)

R28-29: 1 hdc in each st around. (60)

R30: *2 hdc in next st, 1 hdc in each of next 9 sts*, repeat from* 6 times. (66)

R31-32: 1 hdc in each st around. (66)

DIY Spooky Crochet For Adults

R33: *2 hdc in next st, 1 hdc in each of next 10 sts*, repeat from* 6 times. (72)

R34-35: 1 hdc in each st around. (72)

R36: *2 hdc in next hdc, 1 hdc in each of next 11 sts*, repeat from* 6 times. (78)

R39: *1 hdc in each of next 38 sts, 2 hdc in next st*, repeat from* 2 times. (80)

Now, make the brim

R40: Sctfl only in each st around. (80)

R42: *2 hdc in next st, 1 hdc in each of next 10 sts*, repeat from* 8 times. (96)

R43: *2 hdc in next st, 1 hdc in each of next 11 sts*, repeat from* 8 times. (104)

R43: *2 hdc in next st, 1 hdc in each of next 12 sts*, repeat from* 8 times. (112)

R44: *2 hdc in next st, 1 hdc in each of next 13 sts*, repeat from* 8 times. (120)

R45: *2 hdc in next st, 1 hdc in each of next 14 sts*, repeat from* 8 times. (128)

R46: *2 hdc in next st, 1 hdc in each of next 15 sts*, repeat from* 8 times. (136)

R47: *2 hdc in next st, 1 hdc in each of next 16 sts*, repeat from* 8 times. (144)

DIY Spooky Crochet For Adults

R48: *2 hdc in next st, 1 hdc in each of next 17 sts*, repeat from* 8 times. (152)

R49: *2 hdc in next st, 1 hdc in each of next 18 sts*, repeat from* 8 times. (160)

R50: Hdc in each st around. (160)

Fasten off.

DIY Spooky Crochet For Adults

Creepy Candy

Materials:

DROPS NEPAL from Garnstudio

50 g color no 2920, orange

50 g color no 8903, black

DROPS CROCHET Hook size 3 mm / C – or size needed to get 20 sc x 22 rows = 4" x 4" (10 x 10 cm).

ACCESSORIES: Poly stuffing to fill the spider.

PATTERN:

See diagram A.1. Diagram shows basket seen from bottom and out to the sides (side of basket is shown as it was flat).

CROCHET INFO:

Beg every round with 1 ch and finish round with 1 sl st in first ch from beg of round.

WORK 2 SC TOG AS FOLLOWS:

Insert hook in first sc and pull yarn through, insert hook in next sc and pull yarn through, make a YO and pull yarn through all 3 loops on hook.

BASKET:

Worked from bottom up.

Work 4 ch on hook size 3 mm / C with orange and form a ring with 1 sl st in first ch.

ROUND 1: READ CROCHET INFO! Work 6 sc in ch-ring.

ROUND 2: Work 2 sc in every sc = 12 sc.

ROUND 3: Work * 1 sc in first/next sc, 2 sc in next sc *, repeat from *-* the entire round = 18 sc.

ROUND 4: Work * 1 sc in each of the first/next 2 sc, 2 sc in next sc *, repeat from *-* the entire round = 24 sc.

ROUND 5: Work * 1 sc in each of the first/next 3 sc, 2 sc in next sc *, repeat from *-* the entire round = 30 sc.

ROUND 6: Work * 1 sc in each of the first/next 4 sc, 2 sc in next sc *, repeat from *-* the entire round = 36 sc. REMEMBER THE CROCHET GAUGE!

Continue by working 1 sc more between inc until piece measures approx. 12 cm / 4¾" in diameter (if you want a larger basket continue the same way until desired diameter). NOW MEASURE PIECE FROM HERE!

Work 1 sc in every sc until piece measures approx. 4.5 cm / 1 3/4" (or desired height), switch to black and work 2 round with 1 sc in every sc. Work next round as follows: Work * 2 sc in first/next sc, skip 1 sc *, repeat from *-* the entire round. Fasten off.

COB WEB:

Sew on cob web with black - see diagram A.1. First sew the vertical lines that go around the middle, then sew evenly, beg in first round with sc in black. Then sew the diagonal lines in 3 rounds.

Beg the vertical lines with 1 stitch at the beg of round (- see arrow in diagram), sew 1 stitch in the middle of bottom, sew through edge, baste on the back, sew through edge, sew 1 stitch in the middle of bottom etc. the entire round - NOTE: Make sure that to avoid a tight yarn. Then sew the diagonal lines (= 3 round), sew 1 backstitches around each of the vertical lines in the crossing point to fasten the vertical lines. Fasten yarn after last round.

SPIDER:

BODY:

Beg at the back of body and work forward.

Work 4 ch on hook size 3 mm / C with black and form a ring with 1 sl st in first ch. READ CROCHET INFO!

ROUND 1: Work 6 sc in ch-ring.

ROUND 2: Work 2 sc in every sc the entire round = 12 sc.

ROUNDS 3-6: 1 sc in every sc. REMEMBER THE CROCHET GAUGE!

ROUND 7: Work all SC TOG 2 by 2 - see explanation above. = 6 sc.

HEAD:

ROUND 8: Work * 1 sc in first/next sc, 2 sc in next sc *, repeat from *-* the entire round = 9 sc.

ROUND 9: Work 1 sc in every sc.

ROUND 10: Work 1 sc in first sc, then work all sc tog 2 by 2 = 5 sc.

Put some poly stuffing in the spider, cut the yarn. Sew on 2 eyes with stitches in orange. Baste it up and down around the opening at the top of head and tighten.

Twine a black yarn around the transition between body and head, fasten.

LEGS:

Work 4 pairs of legs in black (= 8 legs in total). Beg with the longest legs at the back. Work legs tog in the middle so that they are easy to fasten under the spider.

The 2 legs at the back: Work 21 ch, cut the yarn.

The 2 second to last legs: Work 10 ch, then 1 sl st in the middle ch from previous ch row and 10 ch, cut the yarn.

The 2 second foremost legs: Work 9 ch, then 1 sl st in sl st from previous ch row and 9 ch, cut the yarn.

The 2 front legs: Work 8 ch, then 1 sl st in sl st from previous ch row and 8 ch, cut the yarn.

To avoid fastening the strands in each end of legs, tie a small knot right by the ch row, then cut the yarn directly below the knot.

Place all legs under the spider and fasten them on the middle.

If you want to hang the spider, make a loop by pulling a yarn through the middle of body and back, let the loop be approx. 6 cm / 2 3/8" long, tie the 2 strands tog under the body and fasten.

Diagram

All measurements in charts are in cm.

= middle of bottom

= round with diagonal lines (sew around crossing point for vertical line)

= vertical lines

= basting stitch on the back

= inner circle (= bottom) and the 2 outer circles (= edge in black)

= 3 sc-rows between each stitch

= 5 sc-rows between each stitch

= beg of round

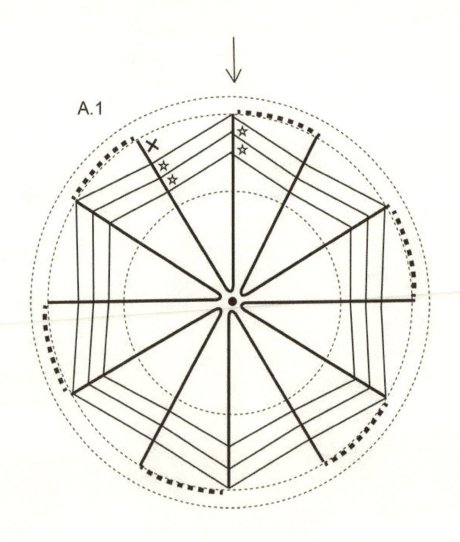

www.ingramcontent.com/pod-product-compliance
Lightning Source LLC
LaVergne TN
LVHW041232050125
800559LV00036B/769